Trailblazers in Frozen Worlds

capstone
classroom

BTR Zone (Bridge to Reading) is published by Capstone Classroom,
1710 Roe Crest Drive, North Mankato, Minnesota 56003
www.capstoneclassroom.com

ISBN: 978-1-62521-026-5

Editorial Credits

Abby Colich, editor; Kazuko Collins, layout artist; Eric Gohl, media researcher

Photo Credits

Alamy: DIZ Muenchen GmbH, Sueddeutsche Zeitung Photo, 30, Everett
Collection Inc., 4, 10, Mary Evans Picture Library, 14; AP Photo: 24–25, Comic
Relief/Mike Carling, 37, Obed Zilwa, 28, PA Wire/Martin Hartley, 35; Corbis:
Bettmann, 8, 13, 17, 21, 22, 33, Galen Rowell, 38; Library of Congress: cover,
7; Newscom: EPA/YONHAP, 43, KRT/Mark McDonald, 27; Wikipedia: Daniel
Leussler, 40–41, Henry Bowers, 19

Design Elements: Shutterstock

About the Cover

Chief Petty Officer Edgar Evans, shown during the British Antarctic
Expedition in 1910 or 1911.

Printed in the United States of America in North Mankato, Minnesota.
072014   008282R

TABLE OF
CONTENTS

Dark Days

Imagine that nighttime does not exist. The sun is always
up and shining. How would you know when to go to bed?
How would you sleep with the sun shining in your window?
This is what it is like for half of the year at the North Pole.
During the other half of the year, it's dark for six months.
How do you think your body would react to such dark days?

CHAPTER 1

Top of the World

Imagine that everything around you looks white. The land, the animals, and even your breath are white. It is also cold all the time. This is what the **North Pole** is like.

There are no hills or mountains at the North Pole. There is only snow and ice as far as the eyes can see.

Few places on Earth are as harsh as the North Pole. During winter the average temperature is -29° Fahrenheit (-34° Celsius). Now that's cold! You don't need a swimsuit when you visit the North Pole. The average temperature in the summer is 32°F (0°C)

Blizzards can happen at any time. And they can last for days!

Why would anyone want to go to such a place? The answer is simple. Humans want to learn all they can about their world.

North Pole · the northern most point of the Earth

blizzard · a storm with dry, driving snow, strong winds, and intense cold

Robert Peary: First Man to Reach the North Pole

Do you like being first to do things? Many **explorers** across the world wanted to reach the North Pole first. The race was on!

Robert Peary was an American explorer. He was born in 1856. He traveled around the world. Peary discovered that Greenland was an island.

But Peary wanted to do more. He had a desire to learn about other lands. He wanted to see lands that no one else had seen. He wanted to be the first person to set foot on the top of the world.

Robert Peary aboard his ship, the *Roosevelt*

explorer · a person who travels in search of new information

Matthew Henson

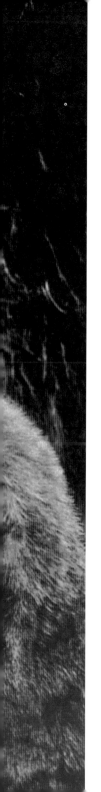

Matthew Henson: True Friend and Companion

Have you ever had a true friend? Did you do everything with that friend? Robert Peary and Matthew Henson had that kind of friendship.

Henson also had a wish to travel the world. What made their friendship so rare? Henson was an African-American. Peary was not. Such friendships were not common in those days. Together they would reach their goal. They would be the first people to walk on the North Pole.

Peary and Henson knew they would have to learn how to live in the harsh Arctic weather.

To prepare Peary and Henson lived with **Inuits**. The Eskimos had always lived in the cold Arctic. Peary and Henson learned how to build **igloos** to sleep in and how to hunt for food. They learned to drive dogsleds. They could stay warm in the cold.

The Inuits taught them a lot. Peary and Henson were now ready to go to the North Pole.

Inuit · native people living in cold northern places like the state of Alaska

igloo · a house usually built of blocks of hard snow

9

Members of Robert Peary's team planted an American flag when they reached the North Pole.

Reaching the North Pole

It took Peary and Henson several tries to reach their goal. They started their first trip to the North Pole in 1893. They had to turn back. They tried again in 1898. Again they failed. They started their third trip in 1905. It was wintertime. The ice was firm. It was the coldest part of the year.

They sailed on an American ship named *Roosevelt*. They formed a team. They took 246 dogs. They took a lot of equipment and food.

The explorers went as far as they could on the ship. Eventually ice blocked their path. They then used the dogs and sleds. Along the way, men and dogs were left behind. They needed to save food.

Peary, Henson, and four Inuit men made it to the top of the world. It was April 6, 1909. They planted an American flag.

What an honor! Peary received a lot of attention for reaching his goal. Henson did not. Many believed this was because Henson was African-American.

Peary died in Washington, D.C., in 1920. He was 63 years old. He was buried in Arlington National Cemetery.

After the trip, Henson worked at the New York Customs House. He also went to college. In 1944 he received the Congressional Medal of Honor.

When Henson died in 1955, he was buried in a simple grave. But in 1988 he was moved to Arlington National Cemetery. He now lies beside his friend Robert Peary.

Henson shows the route he and Peary took to the North Pole on this map.

Roald Amundsen studies
a map of the Antarctic.

The Great Race Ends in Death

The North Pole had been reached. What was left to be explored? People turned their attention to the **South Pole**. This pole is harder to reach. It is located on the **continent** of Antarctica.

This large piece of land is covered with snow and ice. The land slopes upward. As you climb, the air gets cooler.

Roald Amundsen

Roald Amundsen of the country of Norway had been on his way to the North Pole. He stopped when he heard that Peary had reached it first. Amundsen turned his focus to the South Pole.

Robert Falcon Scott of England also wanted to be the first person to reach the South Pole. A new race was on!

South Pole · the southern most point of the Earth
continent · one of earth's seven large land masses

15

Robert F. Scott

Robert F. Scott of England was born in 1868. Members of his family had been sailors. He wanted to be one too. He was chosen to go to the South Pole for England.

Scott had a much harder time reaching the South Pole than Amundsen. He used gas-powered sleds. Motor vehicles were a new **invention**. Scott also brought a lot of men with him. He also took ponies. This meant he had to bring a lot of supplies.

His first attempt to reach the South Pole failed. On his second try, he sailed on a ship called *Terra Nova*. He took 19 ponies with him on the ship.

Scott realized that his men did not know how to drive the gas-powered sleds. They had to learn how to drive them in the snow.

Bad weather on the trip caused many problems. The ponies got stuck in the soft snow. They became too tired to go on. **Frostbite** (injury to the skin from the cold) became a problem. It was on the men's toes and noses. Men and horses had to be left behind. So did supplies.

invention · a new idea or machine

frostbite · injury to any part of the body from the extreme cold

Scott and his team of men used ponies in their try to reach the South Pole.

On January 17, 1912, Scott and four of his men made it to the South Pole! But their joy did not last long. At the South Pole, they found a Norwegian flag. It had been planted by Amundsen. Amundsen had arrived there on December 14, 1911. Scott and his team had lost the race by five weeks.

The return trip was terrible. Scott, along with the four men, met horrible storms. They ran out of food. The men became weak and ill.

One of the men, Petty Officer Edgar Evans, had very bad frostbite. He died on February 17. Scott and his crew buried their friend in the deep snow.

Later another one of the men, Captain L. E. G. Oates, became too frostbitten to continue. He begged Scott to go on without him. But Scott and the others would not leave their friend. One night after everyone had gone to bed, Oates walked out into the night. He was never seen again.

Scott (sitting center) and the other four men at their camp in the Antarctic in January 1912

Scott and the two remaining men were left to continue the trip. Eleven miles (18 kilometers) from the last station, a bad blizzard came upon them. It lasted for days. They could not continue in the snow and wind.

The men sat and waited. But the cold and the lack of food made it impossible to continue. **Historians** (history experts) believe that Scott died on March 29, 1912.

Eight months later, Scott and his two friends were found. They had died in their tent. Scott was the last to die.

Scott was not the first person to reach the South Pole. Even so, he was greatly honored because of his bravery. Unlike Amundsen, Scott did more than run the race to the South Pole. He also collected useful **data** (information) about the "bottom" of the world. He proved how you run the race is also important.

What became of Amundsen? He never received the honor or wealth he thought he had earned. But he continued to travel to the South Pole. On June 18, 1928, he died in a plane crash.

The burial site of Scott, Wilson, and Bowers in the Antarctic

Louise Boyd became
known as "The Girl
Who Tamed the Arctic."

CHAPTER 3

Trailblazing Women

Louise Boyd: "The Girl Who Tamed the Arctic"

Is exploring just for men? No! In the early 1900s, women gained more rights and freedoms. One of these women was Louise Boyd.

Boyd was born in the state of California in 1887. She had a rich family. She enjoyed playing with her two brothers. But her brothers were often sick. They died when Boyd was a teenager. By the time she was 33 years old, both of her parents had also died. Boyd **inherited** (received) a lot of money.

Boyd did not have close family members. She traveled the world. She wanted to do something important with her life and her money.

Boyd traveled to the Arctic. She fell in love with the beauty of the area. She learned to hunt polar bears. She took pictures with her camera. She wanted to learn more about this great **frontier**.

inherit · to receive money from someone, usually after their death

frontier · the furthest limit of a country, usually with no people living there

In 1928 Boyd visited the country of Norway. While there, she learned about Umberto Nobile. The Italian explorer had gone to the Arctic region. He was missing. Roald Amundsen had gone looking for Nobile. He too had gotten lost. Boyd decided that she would go and look for Amundsen.

Boyd and her crew spent four months looking for Amundsen. She did not find him. But she returned to a big surprise. Norwegian government leaders gave her an important medal. It was their way of thanking her.

By 1931 Boyd had gone to the Arctic every year. She went with scientists who wanted to know more about the Arctic. Boyd used her own money to pay for these trips.

Boyd's ship, the *Hobby* shown here in Norway.

Boyd took thousands of pictures of the snow and ice. The pictures helped her and others to study the region. Boyd learned a great deal. Her studies included **glaciers** (moving ice) and the Arctic seas.

By 1941 the United States was fighting in World War II (1939–1945). The U.S. government needed information about the Arctic. They also wanted to know more about the North Pole. How did this area affect radios? They turned to Boyd. She collected a lot of information to help the United States.

Boyd hated to fly. But in 1955 she overcame her fear. Boyd became the first woman to fly over the North Pole. She was 68 years old.

glacier · a slow-moving, giant mass of ice

Ann Bancroft: Going to the Head of the Class

In 1955 Ann Bancroft was born in the state of Minnesota. Her family encouraged her wish to be an explorer. At age eight, she was leading camping trips in her backyard.

Bancroft's family liked to take risks. After the fourth grade, her father moved the family to Kenya, Africa. They lived there for two years. Bancroft loved it. She was able to follow her dreams. She had high hopes for her life.

Her family returned to the United States. Bancroft was sad. She could no longer hide the problems she was having in school. Bancroft worked hard, but her grades were low. Teachers found that Bancroft had **dyslexia**, a reading problem. Her teachers took Bancroft out of art and gym classes to help her with reading. Bancroft hated this. She felt like she was being punished.

After Bancroft graduated from high school, she went to college. She became a special education teacher. She wanted to help other children who had problems in school.

Ann Bancroft is a teacher and polar explorer.

dyslexia · a reading problem associated with eyesight and hearing

Bancroft pulls a sled
behind her in Antarctica.

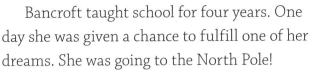

Bancroft taught school for four years. One day she was given a chance to fulfill one of her dreams. She was going to the North Pole!

In 1986 Bancroft and five male team members made it to the North Pole. They used dogsleds on the 56-day trip. Ann became the first woman to reach the top of the world. This was a great success for a kid who had problems in school!

But Bancroft did not stop doing great things. In 1992–1993 she led an all-women team to the South Pole. This was another dream come true. This made Bancroft the first woman to go to both the North and South poles.

Bancroft continues to inspire and help people today. She is the founder of Let Me Play. This group supports teenage girls in sports.

Bancroft wants to help children everywhere to dream big. She believes that dyslexia, being poor, or any situation should not stop dreams!

Salomon Andrée attempted to fly over the North Pole in a hot air balloon

CHAPTER 4

Crossing Frozen Wastelands

How would you travel to the North Pole? Would you use skis or dogsleds? Or would you travel the way S. A. Andrée did?

Salomon August Andrée

Salomon August Andrée was born in the country of Sweden in 1854. He became a pilot of hot air balloons. He had been reading about the trips to the North Pole. He thought he could do better. Rather than using dogs and sleds, he would use a balloon to fly there.

Andrée built a 97-foot (30-meter) tall balloon. It was made out of silk. It used **hydrogen** to float in the air. Andrée's plan was to fly in a straight line right over the North Pole.

He and his crew of two men set off in their balloon on July 11, 1897. Their hopes were flying high, just like their balloon.

The trip began badly. Then it got worse. There was no way to steer the balloon. The hydrogen that kept the balloon in the air began to leak. They could not fly high enough to get above the **fog** and clouds.

The balloon crashed after just three days. What a let down!

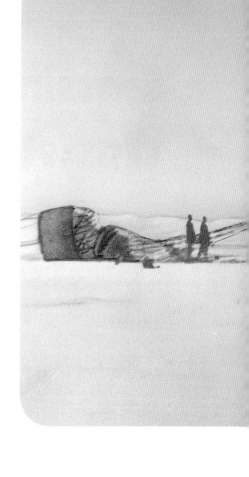

Years later the remains of the balloon were found. The men had kept diaries. They wrote that no one had been hurt in the accident. They had been only 300 miles (483 kilometers) from the North Pole. But they were unable to go on. The men had turned back.

They became too tired to travel. Historians believe they died in October 1897.

A member of Andrée's team took this photo of the balloon after it crashed.

Ben Saunders

Ben Saunders was born in England in 1977. He did not do well in school. His teachers did not think he would amount to much. But he has proven them wrong.

Saunders is a polar explorer. He loves going to the Arctic region. He likes learning how people can survive in a cold, harsh region.

On his first trip to the North Pole, Saunders did not reach his goal. Many saw this as a failure. But Saunders saw it as a way to learn more. Saunders has since learned that trips to the North Pole are not all about speed. They are also about **endurance**. Who can last the longest? It is not easy to live in a frozen world. Everywhere you look is snow and ice. There is no other life to be seen except polar bears.

In 2004 Saunders became the third person to go to the North Pole alone. He was also the youngest. Not only did he travel **solo**, but he also walked much of the way.

endurance · ability to bear pain and hardship

solo · a person who acts or performs alone

Saunders sets out on an attempt to reach the North Pole.

Saunders usually travels alone. So how can we be sure he has done what he claims? He **blogs**! Through the **Internet**, people can travel with Saunders. It may not be quite as exciting as actually going to the Arctic. But it's a lot easier—and warmer—than battling the ice and snow!

blog · to write an online journal

Internet · a system that allows people to share information with others through computers

35

Helen Skelton

Helen Skelton was born July 19, 1983. She grew up in a rural (countryside) area of England. After college she became a **journalist** (person who writes for a magazine or newspaper).

In 2008 Skelton joined the children's television show *Blue Peter*. On the show she **interviews** interesting people. She also talks about fun things to do. In January 2012 she did something special.

To help raise money for Sport Relief, Skelton went to the South Pole. Sport Relief is a charity, a group that helps people in need. It took Skelton 18 days to get to the pole. She did not use dogs or sleds. She used skis and a kite. She also used an ice bike. Skelton was the first person to reach the South Pole by bicycle. She was 28 years old.

Guinness World Records gave Skelton an award for being the first person to travel 62 miles (100 kilometers) while kite-skiing. She traveled the distance in 7 hours and 28 minutes.

Why did Skelton do it? She wanted to be an example to younger explorers. Skelton knows there are still plenty of new adventures in the world. Find your dare and go for it!

journalist · a person who writes for a magazine or newspaper

interview · to ask someone questions to find out more about something

Helen Skelton was the first person in the world to reach the South Pole by bicycle.

CHAPTER 5

Today's Trailblazers

Not long ago only a few animals lived in Antarctica. Today a few people have buildings there.

Most of the buildings are used for scientific study. Scientists and explorers live in them. They are found all over Antarctica.

The first research stations were made of wood and built on rock. Construction had to be quick. Good weather does not last long in Antarctica.

Today's research stations are made with materials that can withstand the harsh weather. Some of the stations are on **stilts**, or posts supporting the building. This keeps the melting spring snow out of the stations.

People live in some of the stations year-round. Other stations only have summer visitors. But all of the stations have up-to-date equipment and technology.

stilts · posts supporting a structure built over land or water　**39**

Amundsen-Scott South Pole Station

The first **permanent** structure on Antarctica was the Amundsen-Scott South Pole Station. The United States built it in 1957.

This station has been rebuilt several times. Today it is a very new structure. It uses new ways to keep power and supplies ready for use. It also has a small **greenhouse**. Vegetables are grown there. Without the greenhouse, the people at the station would not have any food for winter.

The Amundsen-Scott South Pole Station is located at the bottom of the world.

permanent · lasting a long time or forever

greenhouse · building in which temperature is controlled to raise plants and vegetables

Interview with Dr. Jesse Purdy

Southwestern University, Georgetown, Texas; October 27, 2012

Talk about your trips to Antarctica. When did you go?

Dr. Purdy: I went to Antarctica in 2001 and 2002. On both trips I arrived around October 1 and returned by December 10. It is springtime in Antarctica at this time.

Where did you stay?

Dr. Purdy: The United States has three stations on Antarctica. McMurdo Station is the largest. It is open year-round. It has everything you need.

Did you stay at McMurdo Station the entire time you were on Antarctica?

Dr. Purdy: No. From McMurdo we went to Ross Island looking for the seals. There we stayed in tents on the ice.

Why did you want to study seals?

Dr. Purdy: There are not too many animals that live at Antarctica. The Weddell seals are known for being very vocal. They like to "talk" a lot. My team and I wanted to see if we could start understanding what they are saying.

How did you do this?

Dr. Purdy: First we dug a large hole in the ice. Holes in the ice are very important to the seals. It lets them get air. It was also how we watched the seals underwater. Underwater they catch the fish they eat.

Next we caught a few female seals. We put little computers on their bellies. We could tell where the females went and how fast they traveled. We could also tell how much they needed to eat and how much they ate.

We wanted to see who they were talking to when they made the sounds they make. Were they asking for help? Were they fighting? Were they playing games?

With all that snow, ice, and cold temperatures, how did you enjoy your trip to Antarctica?

Dr. Purdy: I loved it! I would love to go back again. There is so much to learn there!

43

Read More

Dowdeswell, Evelyn, et al. *Scott of the Antarctic.* Chicago: Heinemann Library, 2013.

Hanel, Rachael. *Can You Survive Antarctica?: An Interactive Survival Adventure.* Survival. Mankato, Minn.: Capstone Press, 2012.

Wade, Mary Dodson. *Amazing Arctic Explorer Matthew Henson.* Amazing Americans. Berkeley Heights, N.J.: Enslow Publishers, 2012.

Internet Sites

FactHound offers a safe, fun way to find Internet sites related to this book. All of the sites on FactHound have been researched by our staff.

Here's all you do:
Visit *www.facthound.com*
Type in this code: 9781625210265

Check out projects, games and lots more at
www.capstonekids.com

Glossary
of Text Features

Text Feature	How to Use It
Caption: A word or group of words shown with a picture or illustration	Read a caption to understand information that may not be in the text.
Diagram: A drawing that shows or explains something	Examine a diagram to understand steps in a process, how something is made, or the parts of something.
Glossary: List of key terms with their meanings	Look up key terms in the glossary to find their meanings and to get a better understanding of the topic of the text.
Index: Alphabetical list of key terms, names, and topics in a text with their page numbers	Use the index to find pages that contain information you are looking for.
Map: A drawing that represents a place, such as a country or city	Use a map to understand relative locations and determine where events took place.
Photograph or Illustration: Visuals that are created by cameras or drawn	Examine photographs and illustrations to better understand ideas in the text that might be unclear.
Subhead: Word or group of words that divides the text into sections and tells the main idea of a section	Use subheads to locate information in the text and understand how a text is organized.
Table: Represents data in a small space	Examine a table to understand data or to compare information in the text.
Table of Contents: List of the major parts of the book and their page numbers	Use a table of contents to locate general information in the text and see how the topics are organized.
Text Box: A box in the text that provides extra information about a topic	Read a text box to understand interesting or important information.
Text Style: Bold, color, or italic words in the text	Pay attention to bold, italic, and color words to figure out which words in the text are important.
Timeline: Shows events in the order in which they occurred	Use a timeline to understand the order in which events occurred or how one event led to another.

Glossary

blizzard (BLIZ-urd) · a storm with dry, driving snow, strong winds, and intense cold

blog (BLOG) · write an online journal

continent (KAHN-tuh-nuhnt) · one of earth's seven large land masses

data (DAY-tuh) · facts and information

dyslexia (dis-LEK-see-uh) · a reading problem associated with eyesight and hearing

endurance (en-DUR-enss) · ability to bear pain and hardship

explorer (ik-SPLOR-uhr) · a person who travels in search of new information

fog (FOG) · water floating in the air

frontier (fruhn-TIHR) · the furthest limit of a country, usually with no people living there

frostbite (FRAWST-bite) · injury to any part of the body from exposure to extreme cold

glacier (GLAY-shur) · a slow-moving, giant mass of ice

greenhouse (GREEN-houss) · building in which temperature is controlled to raise plants and vegetables

historian (hi-STAWR-ee-uhn) · expert in history

hydrogen (HAHY-druh-juhn) · colorless gas

igloo (IG-loo) · a dome-shaped house, usually built of blocks of hard snow

inherit (in-HER-it) · to receive from someone, usually after their death

Internet (IN-tur-net) · a system that allows people to share information with others through computers

interview (IN-tur-vyoo) · to ask someone questions to find out more about something

Inuit (IN-oo-it) · native people living in cold northern places like the sate of Alaska

invention (in-VEN-shuhn) · a new idea or machine

journalist (JUR-nl-ist) · a person who writes for a magazine or newspaper

North Pole (NORTH POHL) · the northern most point of the Earth

permanent (PUR-muh-nuhnt) · lasting a long time or forever

solo (SOH-loh) · a person who acts or performs alone

South Pole (SOUTH POHL) · the southern most point of the Earth

stilts (STILTSS) · posts supporting a structure built over land or water

Index